DeMarcus Cousins

KINGS

15

THE STORY OF THE SACRAMENTO KINGS

Harrison Barnes

A HISTORY OF HOOPS

THE STORY OF THE

SACRAMENTO KINGS

JIM WHITING

Tyreke Evans

CREATIVE EDUCATION / CREATIVE PAPERBACKS

Published by Creative Education and Creative Paperbacks
P.O. Box 227, Mankato, Minnesota 56002
Creative Education and Creative Paperbacks are imprints of
The Creative Company
www.thecreativecompany.us

Design and production by Blue Design (www.bluedes.com)
Art direction by Rita Marshall

Photographs by Corbis, Getty (Bettmann, Lachlan Cunningham, Jonathan
Daniel, Victor Decolongon, Gina Ferazzi, Otto Greule Jr., Thearon W.
Henderson, John Iacono, Icon Sports Wire, Walter Iooss Jr., Jed Jacobsohn,
Fernando Medina, Manny Millan, Layne Murdoch, NBA Photo Library, Dick
Raphael, Steven Ryan, Ezra Shaw, Rocky Widner), © Steve Lipofsky, Newscom
(Ting Shen/Xinhua/Photoshot), US Presswire (David Butler II)

Library of Congress Cataloging-in-Publication Data
Names: Whiting, Jim, 1943- author.
Title: The story of the Sacramento Kings / by Jim Whiting.
Description: Mankato, Minnesota : Creative Education and Creative
  Paperbacks, 2023. | Series: Creative Sports: A History of Hoops |
  Includes index. | Audience: Ages 8-12 |
  Audience: Grades 4-6 | Summary: "Middle grade basketball fans are
  introduced to the extraordinary history of NBA's Sacramento Kings with a
  photo-laden narrative of their greatest successes and losses"-- Provided
  by publisher.
Identifiers: LCCN 2022016921 (print) | LCCN 2022016922 (ebook) | ISBN
  9781640266421 (library binding) | ISBN 9781682771983 (paperback) | ISBN
  9781640007833 (pdf)
Subjects: LCSH: Sacramento Kings (Basketball team)--History--Juvenile
  literature.
Classification: LCC GV885.52.S24 W55 2023 (print) | LCC GV885.52.S24
  (ebook) | DDC 796.323/640979454--dc23/eng/20220523
LC record available at https://lccn.loc.gov/2022016921
LC ebook record available at https://lccn.loc.gov/2022016922

Oscar Robertson

CONTENTS

LEGENDS OF THE HARDWOOD

THE CHICAGO BULLS

Tyreke Evans

A MAJESTIC COMEBACK

Sacramento Kings fans might have been forgiven if they changed channels on their TV sets when their team fell far behind the Chicago Bulls on December 21, 2009. Chicago had enjoyed a near-perfect first quarter. They shot 71% from the field and forced seven turnovers to jump out to a 38–19 lead. They extended the margin to 67–43 at halftime. With 8:50 remaining in the third quarter, they built a seemingly insurmountable 79–44 edge. That was a 35-point difference. Sacramento pecked away at the lead, then ended the quarter with a 19-5 run. Still, the Bulls had a 19-point lead at 88–69.

Sacramento shooting guard Ime Udoka came off the bench to score 15 points in the fourth quarter. His three-pointer at 2:28 sliced the margin to 95–91. Then rookie guard Tyreke Evans scored nine points in a two-minute span to bring Sacramento all the way back and take the lead. The Kings now led 100–98 with 15 seconds left. Shooting guard Beno Udrih sank two free throws to ice Sacramento's 102–98 victory. The Kings had outscored Chicago 33–10 in the final quarter. It was the second-biggest comeback in National Basketball Association (NBA) history.

Kings coach Paul Westphal summarized the epic evening. "It's unheard of to do what just happened," he said. "I'm not even sure I believe it, but it sure was fun."

Getting to this game had taken many years, four different homes, and several name changes. A businessman in Rochester, New York named Les Harrison had been involved in basketball since his high school days in the early 1920s. He founded a team called the Rochester Seagrams. The team played in the 1940 and 1941 World Professional Basketball Championships. Harrison moved

SACRAMENTO KINGS

9

LEGENDS
OF THE HARDWOOD

BOB DAVIES
POINT GUARD
HEIGHT: 6-FOOT-1
ROYALS SEASONS: 1945–55

DOING DOUBLE DUTY

Bob Davies had been a two-time All-American player at Seton Hall University before World War II. After serving in the conflict, he joined the Royals during the 1945–46 season and helped them win the NBL title. He became the team's star player in the following season. He was also the coach at Seton Hall. He guided an undersized Pirates team called the Mighty Midgets to a 24–3 mark. There was just one problem. Rochester was 300 miles away from South Orange, New Jersey where Seton Hall was located. "I took a lot of overnight [train] sleepers," he joked. Sometimes that wasn't enough. He missed 12 of the Royals 44 games due to scheduling conflicts. It is a tribute to his talent that he was still named the league's MVP.

Bob Davies

the team into the 4,200-seat Edgerton Park Sports Arena in 1943 and changed the name to Rochester Pros.

Two years later, the National Basketball League (NBL) invited the team to join. Harrison paid the $25,000 entry fee out of his own pocket. He held a contest to rename the team. Fifteen-year-old Richard Paeth suggested Royals. "What could be more fitting than this as a name for the team Les Harrison is going to send out to bring the crown to Rochester?" he wrote.

The Royals lived up to Paeth's prediction. They won the NBL championship in their first season. Future Hall of Fame guards Al Cervi and Bob Davies led the way. Davies created a sensation for his ballhandling skills. Sportswriter Arthur Daley called him "a blond artist who made the ball obey him."

The Royals played in the league finals the next two years but lost both times. In 1948, Rochester joined the Basketball Association of America (BAA), which was in its third season. They lost in the division finals. The following year, the BAA and NBL merged to form the NBA. Rochester lost in the division semifinals.

In the 1951 playoffs, the Royals beat the Minneapolis Lakers in the Western Division finals. Rochester faced the New York Knicks in the best-of-seven NBA Finals. The Royals won the first three games. New York won the next three. The Knicks held a two-point lead in the decisive Game 7 with two minutes left. Rochester center Arnie Risen hit a free throw and a hook shot. The Royals led 75–74. A New York free throw tied the score. Davies' two free throws and a last-second basket gave the Royals their first NBA championship. Local media praised Harrison. One sportswriter said, "It's been quite an experience for a guy playing around with his own bankroll, stymied by a town which hasn't an adequate-sized arena in which to parade his high-priced and talented performers."

Oscar Robertson

ROYALS IN THE QUEEN CITY

T he sportswriter who praised Harrison noted problems that soon faced the team. Player salaries began rising. The team's arena didn't have enough seats to meet the increased expenses. The Royals began losing. They drafted star rookie forwards Maurice Stokes and Jack Twyman before the 1955–56 season. The downward slide continued. The team won just 31 games that season and the next. Attendance plummeted to just 2,000 fans per game.

Harrison moved the team to Cincinnati, Ohio, in 1957. It seemed an appropriate choice for the Royals. Cincinnati is called "The Queen City." They squeaked into the 1958 playoffs. They lost to the Detroit Pistons in the first round. The team then stumbled to 19 wins in each of the next two seasons. Those losing records gave Cincinnati the top pick in the 1960 NBA Draft. It chose guard Oscar Robertson. Nicknamed "The Big O," Robertson was named NBA Rookie of the Year. "You can't adequately describe him," Twyman said. "It's not any one thing—it's his completeness that amazes you." Robertson led the Royals to the 1963 Eastern Division finals. They lost to the Boston Celtics 4 games to 3.

The Royals drafted center/power forward Jerry Lucas before the 1963–64 season. He also became NBA Rookie of the Year. The Royals marched back to the division finals. Once again, Boston beat them. The Royals remained confident. "We thought it was just a matter of time before we would get our turn," Lucas said.

Maurice Stokes

"Our turn" never came. The Royals suffered first-round playoff defeats in the following three seasons. Starting in 1967–68, the Royals missed the playoffs for five seasons. They drafted quick point guard Nate Archibald in 1970. He became one of the league's scoring leaders. It wasn't enough. The team won only 33 games his rookie year. Their record dropped to only 30 wins in 1971–72. Fans stayed away.

A group of businessmen from Kansas City, Missouri, bought the team. Kansas City's Major League Baseball team was already named Royals. The new owners changed the name to Kings. That way they were still "royal." The team continued to lose. It had one winning record in the first six years in Kansas City. One of the few highlights came in the 1972–73 season. Archibald became the only player to lead the league in both scoring and assists. The Kings traded him three years later.

MAURICE STOKES
POWER FORWARD/CENTER
HEIGHT: 6-FOOT-7
ROYALS SEASONS: 1955–58

JACK TWYMAN
SMALL FORWARD
HEIGHT: 6-FOOT-6
ROYALS SEASONS: 1955–66

THE TRAGEDY OF MAURICE STOKES

Everyone predicted superstardom for Maurice Stokes. He was an All-Star in
each of his first three years. In the final game of the 1957–58 season, his head
hit the floor. He didn't receive proper medical treatment, suffered a seizure,
and became permanently paralyzed. His teammate Jack Twyman became his
legal guardian and took care of him. Stokes died of a heart attack when he
was just 36. "You'll never know, meet, or read about anybody as courageous
as Maurice," said Twyman. Twyman had his own brand of courage. "To do what
he [Twyman] did in the late '50s when, frankly, racial relationships were what
they were, it wasn't a normal thing to do—a white man to basically adopt and
become the legal guardian for Maurice," said John Doleva, president of the
Hall of Fame. The NBA honors the two men with the Twyman-Stokes Teammate
of the Year Award. A vote by players determines the winner.

SACRAMENTO KINGS

15

LEGENDS
OF THE HARDWOOD

Jerry Lucas

JERRY LUCAS
POWER FORWARD
HEIGHT: 6-FOOT-8
ROYALS SEASONS: 1963–69

EARLY BLOOMER

Jerry Lucas started playing basketball for long hours when he was only nine years old. He was always big for his age. While he was in middle school, he played pickup games with college players. In high school, he broke Wilt Chamberlain's national point-scoring record. Many major college teams wanted him. He was an A-student and chose Ohio State. "State was the only school that talked to me first about my education," he said. He led the Buckeyes to three straight national championship games. His run of success continued in the NBA. He was a three-time All-NBA First Team selection who averaged nearly 20 points and 20 rebounds a game.

They tried to rebuild around dynamic young guards Otis Birdsong and Phil Ford in 1978–79. "They're like two peas in a pod," said coach Cotton Fitzsimmons. "They're the guys who keep this team loose, and you have to be loose to play basketball." Ford was NBA Rookie of the Year.

Birdsong and Ford led the team, but Kansas City lost to the Phoenix Suns in the conference semifinals. They lost to Phoenix in the playoffs again the following season. In 1981, the Kings advanced to the Western Conference finals even though their record was just 40–42. But they lost to the Houston Rockets, 4 games to 1.

MOVING EVEN FARTHER WEST

The 1981 season turned out to be the high point for the Kings in Kansas City. They had only one winning record in the next four seasons. Once again, fans stayed away. In 1985, the team moved to Sacramento, California. The Kings were Sacramento's first professional sports team. Fans embraced them. Every game was sold out. Before the home opener, guard Larry Drew was impressed by the crowd's enthusiasm. "People were dressed in tuxedos, and some women were in evening gowns," he said. "They were really getting geared up for their basketball."

The Kings averaged nearly 109 points per game in their first season. Despite winning just 37 games, they made the playoffs. The Rockets easily defeated them in the first round. Then a long dry spell set in. For eight straight seasons, Sacramento couldn't scrape together even 30 wins in a single season.

Perhaps the worst one came in 1990–91. The Kings had four first-round draft choices. Small forward Lionel Simmons would make the NBA All-Rookie First Team, while shooting guard Travis Mays would be on the Second Team. Despite the talent, the Kings dropped their first seven games, including three on the road. Then they traveled to Washington to face the Bullets. They jumped out to a 53–38 halftime lead but gave it all back in the third quarter. The teams were tied with 38 seconds remaining in the game. Yet another rookie—center Duane Causwell—had a three-point play to give Sacramento an 85–82 lead. The Kings won 87–82. Despite the win, power forward Waymon Tisdale said, "We'll take a lot of bumps and lumps this season." He was right. The Kings remained winless away from home for the rest of the season. Their 37 straight road defeats that season—coupled with six more to start the following season—set an NBA record of 43 that still stands.

The Kings finally started making progress in 1994–95. They won 39 games but missed the playoffs. The following season they made the playoffs for the first time in 10 years. The Seattle SuperSonics defeated them in the first round. Then they had two more losing seasons.

The Kings put together their most successful Sacramento season to date in 1998–99. They went 27–23. A dispute between owners and players had shortened the season. The key newcomer was veteran power forward Chris Webber. He led the league in rebounding. Sacramento faced the Utah Jazz in the first round of the playoffs. The Kings won two of the first three games in the best-of-five series. They lost Game 4 by a single point and Game 5 in overtime to be eliminated.

Mitch Richmond

19

MITCH RICHMOND
SHOOTING GUARD
HEIGHT: 6-FOOT-5
KINGS SEASONS: 1991–98

KING MITCH

Mitch Richmond established a reputation as one of the league's best shooters with the Golden State Warriors. He was upset when he got traded to Sacramento. "I just started crying," Richmond said. He asked his agent if he could retire and come back with a different team. Eventually he adjusted. Richmond became Sacramento's first real superstar. He averaged at least 21 points a game during his seven seasons with the team. He was a six-time All-Star. He was named the 1995 All-Star Game's Most Valuable Player. Richmond credited the team's fans. "I will always praise the city of Sacramento and their fans because, even when I didn't want to be there, they still supported me," he said. But the team never had a winning record while he was with them. Sacramento traded him to Washington in 1998.

REACHING THE SUMMIT—ALMOST

The Kings kept winning. They made the playoffs again the next season. They lost a close series to the Los Angeles Lakers in the first round. They did even better in 2000–01. They beat the Suns in the first round. But the Lakers swept them in the second round. "We had something going," Webber said. "We liked playing together and thought it would be just a matter of time as to when we got our championship."

That championship nearly arrived in 2001–02. Sacramento's 61 wins topped the NBA. In the playoffs, the Kings cruised past the Jazz and the Dallas Mavericks in the first two rounds. That set up a memorable Western Conference finals series with the Lakers, who had tied for the league's second-best mark.

The series lived up to expectations. The Kings won two of the first three games. The last four games were each decided in the final moments. The Lakers sank a three-point shot at the buzzer to win Game 4. Sacramento guard Mike Bibby's jump shot with eight seconds left won Game 5. The next game was controversial. Many people felt the referees favored the Lakers. They shot 27 free throws in the final quarter alone. Those points made the difference in a 106–102 Los Angeles victory. Sportswriter Michael Wilbon said, "I wrote down in my notebook six calls that were stunningly incorrect, all against Sacramento, all in the fourth quarter."

Vlade Divac

Despite the loss, the Kings felt confident. Game 7 was at home. It went into overtime. The Kings missed key shots. They turned the ball over. The Lakers won 112–106. "The Kings were the better team tonight, they deserved to win, but somehow we did," said Lakers coach Phil Jackson. The Kings could only watch as the Lakers swept the Nets for the NBA title. "We should have closed it out when we could, but we have many more years of this," guard Mike Bibby said.

Sacramento won 59 games the following season. They faced the Mavericks in the second round of the 2003 playoffs. Webber injured his knee in the second game. The Kings lost the series. Webber missed most of the 2003–04 season. The Kings still won 55 games. Webber was back for the 2004 playoffs. In Game 7 of the second round, the Kings faced the Minnesota Timberwolves. Webber missed a potential game-tying shot at the buzzer. The Kings continued to have winning records in the next two seasons. Both times they lost in the first round of the playoffs. The second time, in 2005–06, would mark their final playoff appearance for the next 16 seasons.

Mike Bibby

24

CHRIS WEBBER
POWER FORWARD
HEIGHT: 6-FOOT-10
KINGS SEASONS: 1998–2005

LEGENDS
OF THE HARDWOOD

A FABULOUS PLAYER

In college, Chris Webber was one of five outstanding
freshmen starters at the University of Michigan known as
the "Fab Five." They sparked the Wolverines to the national
championship game in 1992 and 1993. The Orlando Magic
took Webber with the first overall pick in the 1993 NBA Draft.
They immediately traded him to Golden State. He averaged
17 points a game and was named NBA Rookie of the Year. The
team traded him to Washington. In his four years there, he
averaged at least 20 points a game. Then he was traded to
Sacramento. The Kings made the playoffs every year Webber
was on the roster. He was a four-time All-Star and made the
All-NBA Team five years in a row.

STAYING PUT

y the 2006–07 season, the key players from the glory days were gone. The Kings won just 33 games. They missed the playoffs for the first time in nine years. They hit bottom two seasons later. Their 17–65 mark was the worst in team history. The Kings struck gold in the 2009 NBA Draft with shooting guard Tyreke Evans. He became the first Sacramento player in more than 30 years to win the Rookie of the Year award. They added center DeMarcus Cousins in the following NBA Draft. He was named to the NBA All-Rookie First Team and quickly blossomed into the face of the franchise.

The Kings took guard Jimmer Fredette in the 2011 NBA Draft. He had been National College Player of the Year. President Barack Obama was among the legion of fans of "Jimmermania." He said, "Best scorer obviously in the country. Great talent." Fredette proved to be a big-time scorer—in the team store. His number 7 jersey was a top seller. Unfortunately, the number also referred to the average number of points he scored per game. That was far short of what the team had hoped for. He lasted less than three seasons.

The Kings went 22–44 in the lockout-shortened 2011-12 season and 28–54 in 2012–13. They played under the threat of moving. A group of Seattle businessmen appeared to have purchased the team. It seemed likely that the Kings would again be playing in a "Queen City." That is one of Seattle's nicknames. Led by Mayor Kevin Johnson—a three-time All-Star with the Phoenix Suns—Sacramento

ISAIAH THOMAS
POINT GUARD
HEIGHT: 5-FOOT-9
KINGS SEASONS: 2011–14

SILENCING THE DOUBTERS

The 2011 NBA Draft wasn't a total loss. The Kings took 5-foot-9 point guard Isaiah Thomas with the 60th and final overall pick. Many people thought that the Kings had wasted the pick. They thought he was too small. Not Thomas. He had confidence in himself. Growing up, he traveled throughout the Tacoma, Washington area with his father for pickup games with grown men. At the University of Washington, he was Pac-10 Freshman of the Year in 2009 and All-Pac-10 First Team the next two years. Much of his success came from his fierce competitive spirit. "People still say I can't play at this level, and I won't be in the league that long," he said. "All of that motivates me." Thomas quickly silenced his doubters. Twice he was named NBA Rookie of the Month. No other 60th pick had received that honor.

Domantas Sabonis

fought back. The NBA owners voted to reject the offer. Eventually, a group promising to keep the Kings in Sacramento made a successful bid.

The increased off-court stability didn't help on the court. Sacramento won just 28 and 29 games the following two seasons. The Kings enjoyed a five-game winning streak midway through the 2015–16 season. At that point they would have been the number-eight seed in the Western Conference. They couldn't maintain the pace. They finished with just 33 wins. That was eight games out of the final playoff spot.

The Kings had a 30–26 mark just before the All-Star break in 2018–19. Once again, they couldn't hold it. They lost six of their last eight games to finish 39–43. Still, it was the best record since their last playoff appearance in 2005–06.

They fell back to 31–41 marks in the next two seasons. With their 30–52 record in 2021–22, the Kings missed the playoffs for the 16th season in a row. That set a new NBA record. They picked up two-time All-Star power forward/center Domantas Sabonis at the trade deadline. He averaged nearly 19 points and more than 12 rebounds per game. He teamed with veteran point guard De'Aaron Fox—who averaged more than 23 points per game—to provide a reliable inside/outside combination. In the 2022 NBA Draft, Sacramento added Iowa power forward Keegan Murray with the fourth overall selection. Murray won the Karl Malone Award as the nation's top power forward. He raised his scoring average from 7.2 points a game as a freshman to 23.5 points a game as a sophomore.

No team in the NBA has endured a longer championship drought than the Kings. Its only NBA title came in 1951. The team was among the most powerful franchises during its early years. Some of the greatest players in the game have been part of the franchise. Kings fans hope the team can return to its former glory. They look forward to another championship banner.

De'Aaron Fox

INDEX